I0819118

LIVING IN ENLIGHTENMENT

LIVING IN ENLIGHTENMENT

A Guided Journal

SADHGURU

HARMONY
NEW YORK

January

JAN 1

ETERNITY

This moment is eternity. How are you going to escape it, even if you try?

JAN 2

JOY FROM WITHIN

Human folly is that people are always trying to extract joy from the outside. You may use the outside as a stimulus or trigger, but the real thing always comes from within.

SIMPLICITY

JAN
3

Let us not make hard work of the simple aspects of life.

DESTINY

JAN
4

Karma is about becoming the source of one's own creation. In shifting responsibility from heaven to oneself, one becomes the very maker of one's destiny.

JAN 5

MEDITATION

All that moves will exhaust itself. Only that which is still, is for always. Meditation is essentially to move toward that stillness, to become like the core of existence.

JAN 6

BITTERNESS

The bitterness of any experience is not in what has happened. The bitterness of any experience is in terms of how you have received it.

MAGIC

JAN 7

There is magic everywhere. If you learn how to live it, life is nothing short of a daily miracle.

HERE AND NOW

JAN 8

If you transcend the limitations of your conscious mind, everything is here and now. It is not like going from this point to that point. *This* point is everything.

JAN 9

ENLIGHTENMENT

If you're capable of ignorance, you're also capable of Enlightenment.

JAN 10

HAPPINESS

Happy people are loosely attached to life. Miserable people cling to life more than anyone else. The more miserable they are, the more they cling to everything around them.

“

TODAY, MODERN SCIENCE IS TELLING YOU THAT EVERYTHING IS THE SAME ENERGY MANIFESTING ITSELF IN A MILLION DIFFERENT WAYS. IF THAT IS SO, WHAT YOU CALL THE DIVINE, WHAT YOU CALL A STONE, WHAT YOU CALL A MAN OR A WOMAN, WHAT YOU CALL A DEMON, ARE ALL THE SAME ENERGY FUNCTIONING IN DIFFERENT WAYS.

”

JAN
11

LIFE

Ultimately, life is neither suffering nor bliss. It is what you make it.

JAN
12

TRANSFORMED

Whatever you eat, drink, and breathe is energy. Whether you transform it into physical, mental, or life energy is up to you. Energy is neither created nor destroyed, it is only transformed.

DREAMS

JAN 13

If your dreams come true, there is nothing terribly special about that. My wish is that your dreams should be *shattered*. Only then will something larger than memory manifest in your life.

HURDLES

JAN 14

Whatever you accept becomes a part of you. Whatever you do not accept stands apart like a huge hurdle.

JAN 15

PAIN AND PLEASURE

You must learn to handle pain in the same way you handle pleasure.

JAN 16

PERCEPTION

The human predicament is just this: *The very seat of your experience is within you, but your perception is entirely outward bound.*

LOST

JAN 17

I want you to get lost! I want to invite you to that place of borderless ignorance—that the ancients have called enlightenment—and the only way to get there is to lose yourself.

START FRESH

JAN 18

We do not want to live out recycled lives. We want to start fresh. We want to write our own scripts.

JAN 19

SEPARATENESS

Unfortunately, our idea of individuality is separateness, and that is the basis of all suffering.

JAN 20

THE LEAP

The leap is worth it. The leap is everything. With the leap, the bottomless abyss becomes boundless freedom.

FEARLESS

JAN 21

Courageous people do idiotic things. Fearful people do little. Fearless people see life as it is and do what is needed.

SELF

The more you identify with your mind, the further away you are from your Self.

JAN 23

COMPASSION

Passion is focused on one thing, therefore it burns out at some point. Compassion is all-inclusive—it has so much fuel to burn that it does not die out.

JAN 24

LOVE

For a person for whom love means everything, everything else is secondary; being alive itself is secondary.

SOCIAL LEARNINGS

JAN 25

Your idea of good and bad has been taught to you. You have imbibed it from the social atmosphere in which you have lived.

TRADITIONS

JAN 26

No tradition, however time-honored, deserves to live on as anything more than a museum piece if it has outlived its relevance.

"

ONCE YOU ARE EMBODIED AND YOU'RE HERE AS A HUMAN BEING, YOU CAN EITHER EVOLVE OR REGRESS. BOTH ARE POSSIBLE FOR YOU. THAT'S THE BEAUTY OF HAVING AN INTELLECT THAT CAN DISCRIMINATE AND CHOOSE. IT CAN MAKE YOU PROGRESS; IT CAN MAKE YOU REGRESS.

"

LISTEN

JAN

27

The body speaks in many ways.

SEEKING

JAN

28

There is a significant difference between *believing* and *seeking*. *Believing* means you have assumed something that you do not know; *seeking* means you have realized that you do not know.

JAN
29

MEMORY

The one thing that human beings simultaneously suffer from and cherish is memory.

JAN
30

HAPPINESS

If you saw your life as an *expression* of your happiness, rather than as a pursuit of it, you would find you have made a significant paradigm shift.

FREEDOM

JAN 31

Choice is the great human gift; freedom is the great human possibility.

February

PRESENCE

FEB 1

The less rigid your personality, the more powerful your presence.

WHO YOU ARE

What kind of garment you are wearing does not decide who you are right now. What kind of house you are living in does not decide who you are right now. How someone else treats you does not decide who you are right now.

FEB 3

STILLNESS

In reality, there is no such thing as meditation. There is only stillness—many levels of stillness.

FEB 4

STRENGTH

You must understand that whatever situations happen to you in your life, you can either come out of them with greater strength or you can be left broken by them.

FLY

FEB 5

Those who long to leave a footprint shall never fly.

BURDEN

FEB 6

If you carry sixty years of burden with you, you're sixty years old. If you don't carry anything, you're like a newborn.

FEB
7

BEING HUMAN

Being human means to consciously do the best you can for everyone and everything you come in touch with.

FEB
8

ATTENTION

The depth of your attention determines the depth of your experience. If your attention is profound, your experience of life is profound.

“

LIFE IS JUST ONE. NUMBERS ARE ONLY IN YOUR MIND. THERE IS NO SUCH THING IN EXISTENCE. LET US SAY THERE IS A POND FULL OF WATER AND YOU DIP YOUR BUCKET IN AND TAKE WATER OUT OF IT. CAN YOU SAY THAT I HAVE TAKEN THIS PARTICULAR WATER . . .

”

FEB
9

A PROCESS

As a human, you are not a *being*, you are a *becoming*, an ongoing process. Nothing is fixed—you can be whichever way you want to be.

FEB
10

PAIN

Pain is bad enough; why make it worse with suffering? Suffering is entirely self-created.

LONGING

FEB 11

If you were alone on this planet, what would you want for yourself. If there were nobody or nothing to compare yourself with, what would you truly long for. That should be the main focus of your life.

USE IT

FEB 12

Whatever you have—your skills, your love, your joy, your ingenuity, your ability to do things—please show it now. Do not try to save it for another lifetime.

FEB 13

TRANSFORMATION

You cannot transform the world without transforming the individual.

FEB 14

VOLITION

Life has no inherent quality whatsoever. The choice is always yours. The volition is always yours.

THE YOGI

Conceptual knowledge is the way of the academic. Perceptual knowing is the way of the yogi.

CONSECRATED

FEB
16

The most important thing is that you must live in a consecrated space. Either you consecrate your home or you consecrate your own body so that you constantly live in that sacred space.

FEB 17

SOCIETY

We get the society we deserve.

FEB 18

CONVENIENCE

Once a teaching has become a source of convenience, it is no good.

CONSEQUENCES

If you can joyfully accept any consequence, do whatever you please. But if the consequences matter to you, you must perform conscious action.

ABANDON

Whether you walk or dance, work or play, cook or sing, just do it with total attention and awareness. Or else, do it with total abandon. Both ways, you are closer to creation.

FEB
21

ANTENNA

The body is like an antenna: If you hold it in the right position, it becomes receptive to all there is in existence. If you hold it another way, you will remain absolutely ignorant of everything beyond the five senses.

FEB
22

IN THE MOMENT

You don't have to *try* to be in the moment. You *are* in the moment. *There is nowhere else to be.*

SELF-EXPERIMENT

FEB 23

It is in the laboratory of self-experiment that every question receives its own nonverbal answer.

LIVING WELL

FEB 24

People may believe they are living well, but they are not. They have good homes, good cars, and good clothes, and they think they are living well because other people don't have the same things. This is not living well.

FEB 25

TWO BANKS

The moment you reject death, you also reject life. You think life is right and death is wrong. It is not so. Life is what it is only because death is. A river always happens between two banks.

FEB 26

CONSCIOUSNESS

Consciousness is not a matter of behavior. It is the nature of existence.

INCLUSION

FEB 27

Avoiding something is not freedom from it. Such morality is based on exclusion. Spirituality, on the other hand, is born of inclusion.

ONE

FEB 28/29

What is seemingly many will turn out to be One.

March

SLOWNESS

MAR 1

Existence is not in a hurry.

GROWTH

It is becoming a norm in the world that growth happens only painfully. It can also happen blissfully, but that is when both the body and mind have been prepared.

MAR 3

FALSE CONCLUSIONS

Truth is not a conclusion. If you keep the false conclusions at bay, truth will dawn.

MAR 4

UNDER CONTROL

Your outer life may not be a hundred percent in your control, but your inner life always will be.

SEEING

If you really want to know spirituality, don't look for anything. Seeking is not about looking for something. It is about enhancing your perception, your very faculty of seeing.

BONDAGE

MAR 6

Many people talk of freedom, but they secretly fear it. They feel secure in bondage.

MAR 7

THE KEY

What *is* love then? It is just your own quality. You are only using the other person as a key to open up what is already within you.

MAR 8

UNDERSTANDING

Even if you spend a lifetime, you still won't understand a leaf, an elephant, an ant, or an atom. Everything you cannot grasp is in a higher state of existential intelligence than you are. When you see this—really see this—you are a devotee.

RIGHT THINGS

MAR 9

Unless we do the right things, the right things will not happen to us.

CONSTRAINTS

MAR 10

The walls of self-preservation that you build today are the walls of self-imprisonment tomorrow. Boundaries that you establish in your life as a protection for yourself today will feel like constraints tomorrow.

MAR 11

YOUR CHOICE

This is the fundamental choice you have: Either you learn to live with creation, or you manufacture your own creation in your head.

MAR 12

LIMITATION TO LIBERATION

Humanity now needs to liberate life, rather than control it. From limitation to liberation—this is the way.

INVOLVED

MAR 13

From this moment onward, be consciously involved with everything around you: the food you eat, the water you drink, the earth you walk upon, the air you breathe, the people around you.

INTELLECT

MAR 14

The intellect, which is based on memory, is a wonderful tool. However, *it can only inform, it cannot transform.*

MAR 15

ACTION

Only the person who is capable of being immersed in work knows the true meaning of rest. Only if you have known intense action will you know the bliss of inaction.

MAR 16

CYCLICAL

Everything that is physical is cyclical.

TRANSCEND

MAR 17

Here is an opportunity to transcend all your limitations of thought, emotion, and action. Here is an opportunity to consciously craft yourself to become the creation you want to be.

TRANQUILIZER

MAR 18

Solace is like a tranquilizer—it means you are only getting deeper into entanglement. It will not liberate you.

MAR 19

AWAKENING

Every human is in the process of awakening to their own divinity.

MAR 20

INFECTIOUS

Depression, grief, and joy are all infectious. You have to make up your mind as to what you want to infect the world with.

DISPASSION

MAR 21

In life, one should have passion toward the highest, compassion for all, and dispassion toward oneself.

LIVING IN THE PAST

MAR 22

For most people, what happened yesterday is more real than what is happening right now. They live by memory. When you live by memory, you live with one foot in the land of death and another in the land of life. That is torture!

“

TO LIVE FULLY IS TO ALLOW YOURSELF TO EXPERIENCE SOMETHING TOTALLY. IF YOU ALLOW YOURSELF TO EXPERIENCE HUNGER TOTALLY, IT IS WONDERFUL AND LIBERATING. IF YOU ALLOW YOURSELF TO EXPERIENCE FOOD TOTALLY, IT IS ALSO WONDERFUL AND LIBERATING.

”

BARRIERS

MAR 23

Power, fame, position—anything can become a barrier, but anything can also become an access point. It's not education or wealth that can open or close you, it's just how you relate to them.

A MIRROR

MAR 24

The atomic and the cosmic, the individual and the universal, mirror each other on every level.

MAR
25

CARRYING GOLD

A spiritual person wants to drop all burdens. Whether it's gold or garbage, both are heavy, but the other fools think carrying gold is great.

MAR
26

MIRACLES

Life happens in many different ways. You have limited yourself to just the physical, the logical—physical in experience, logical in thinking. Anything beyond this, you call a miracle.

DOUBT

MAR 27

Doubt is good—it means you are searching for truth. Suspicion is sickness.

LIMITS

MAR 28

In mediocrity, there is comfort, but no joy. In going beyond your limits, there is joy, but maybe no comfort. You have to choose.

MAR 29

PLAYFUL

If you are a little playful with life, every moment is a celebration.

MAR 30

REST

Rest is the basis of all activity. Stillness is the basis of all Dynamism.

IMMENSE

MAR
31

If you think you are big, you become small. If you know you are nothing, you become immense. This is the beauty of being human.

April

LOVE AFFAIR

APR
1

A spiritual process is not a divorce from life. It is an irrevocable love affair with life.

POSSIBILITIES

APR
2

New, challenging situations are possibilities, not problems. A problem would be if nothing new happens to you.

APR 3

WELL-BEING

Your wellness and your illness, your joy and your misery, all come from within. If you want well-being, it is time to turn inward.

APR 4

TINY SPECK

You are a tiny speck in the universe. But this tiny speck has the potential to contain the whole cosmos.

SELF-IMPORTANCE

APR
5

Once you have become too important in your own thought process, you will be like a tyrant, super confident and bombastic. But how many human beings like you and me have come and gone upon the Planet . . .

EXISTENTIAL

APR
6

The existential has no moral compass. It is about life and the ingredients of life, not social or psychological judgments.

APR 7

DISCIPLINE

Discipline does not mean control. It means having the sense to do exactly what is needed.

APR 8

INVESTMENT

It is true that separateness or individuality is fundamentally a myth. However, as long as a person is invested in this myth, the karmic bondage remains. The greater the investment, the greater the karmic bondage.

POTENTIAL

APR
9

To merely eat, sleep, reproduce, and die, you do not need the sophisticated body, mind, and awareness you have been gifted with. If this tremendous gift is not explored, it is a terrible shame.

INNER EXPERIENCE

APR
10

Repeating a scriptural truth without an inner experience of it is a futile exercise. It will not transform your life in any way.

APR 11

PEACE AND JOY

Most people think peace and joy are the goals of the spiritual life. This is a fallacy. Peace and joy are the basic requirements for a life of well-being.

APR 12

FAILURE

Life knows no failure. Failure exists only for those who are always comparing themselves with others.

“

CONSCIOUSNESS
IS A QUALITY,
NOT A SUBSTANCE.
IT IS THE
NATURE OF
THE COSMOS.

”

APR 13

ASPIRATION

Whatever you feel deprived of looks like the highest aspiration.

APR 14

FORGIVENESS

To forgive does not mean to forget. To forgive means not to carry any bitterness in you, because that destroys your life.

GIVING

APR 15

Fundamentally, the only thing you can give is yourself.

KIN

APR 16

How beautifully you can relate to someone simply depends on your willingness, flexibility, and joyfulness.

APR 17

LINKED

You are inseparably linked to the rest of the universe. Your body already knows that it is part of a great molecular dance of the cosmos. Your mind, however, believes otherwise; it is convinced that it is a limited entity.

APR 18

PREOCCUPATION

When a creation of phenomenal exuberance and grandeur is around you, it is calamitous to live in your own cocoon of preoccupation.

HOMECOMING

APR
19

Enlightenment is not an attainment or an achievement. It is a homecoming.

THE PRESENT

APR
20

The present is your only address. The here and now is your only abode.

APR 21

THE BEAUTY OF LIFE

Try as we might, neither love nor the spiritual process can ever be made utilitarian. They are simply part of the beauty of life. When you try to institutionalize an inner experience, all you are left with is an institution!

APR 22

PATTERNS

The more you have seen something, the less fascinating it becomes. If you see that you have enacted the same patterns again and again, they become less compelling.

CONNECTION

APR 23

Whomever you meet, speak to them like it is the last time you may have that opportunity. It will transform your life.

DISSOLUTION

APR 24

All beings are seeking dissolution, whether they are aware of it or not. Out of their limitations, fears, and misunderstandings, they may think they are not seeking it, but every being is seeking dissolution, always.

APR 25

ENTANGLEMENTS

Whatever it is—illness, death, or any calamity that happens—you can either use it to liberate yourself or you can use it to entangle yourself.

APR 26

A COMPLETE LIFE

This life can interact with, relate to, be with, and include so many things. But still, by itself, it is a complete life.

YOGA

APR 27

How to sit, how to stand, how to breathe, how to do everything, how your heart should beat, how the life within you should pulse—when you pay attention to everything, you are in yoga.

SEEKER

APR 28

A seeker is always young.

APR 29

THE WORLD

Do you want to rule the world or do you want to serve the world? Ultimately, that is the choice.

APR 30

EGO

The ego is always like this: It is not seeing how to be in tune with what's surrounding it. It's trying to stick out. Among people, you want to stick out like a sore thumb, and a sore thumb always hurts.

May

MAY
1

DISPASSION

People have understood dispassion as becoming dry and senseless. Dispassion is not dry and senseless; dispassion means that the bondage with life is gone. Freedom has come.

MAY
2

EXPERIENCE

It is not the amount of action but the depth of experience that makes life rich and fulfilling.

GOD

MAY 3

There is so much talk of God and heaven mainly because human beings have not realized the immensity of being human.

THE EARTH

MAY 4

The body responds the moment it is in touch with the earth. When it is allowed to forget its origins, the body often starts making fanciful demands; when it is constantly reminded, it knows its place.

MAY
5

THE WAY OF THINGS

Karma is not a doctrine. It is not a creed, a scripture, an ideology, a philosophy, or a theory. It is simply the way things are, of cause and effect.

MAY
6

A MESS

If a human being says, "I don't know something," then the possibility of knowing is open in his life. If he believes he knows something that he does not know, he is a mess.

DUALITY

MAY
7

Existence is a dance between the unmanifest and the manifest.

DEVOTION

MAY
8

Devotion can be very beautiful, joyous, ecstatic, but without the clarity of knowing, it could lead to stagnation. On the other hand, without emotion, spiritual practices can become barren, dry, and lifeless.

MAY 9

SELF-PRESERVATION

Only when the gnawing anxiety of self-preservation is completely eliminated from your mind would you dare to explore life. Otherwise, you only want to protect it.

MAY 10

BEQUEST

It is up to us to decide the nature of our bequest to the planet.

BLAME

MAY
11

Your old karma is not the problem. The problem is that your present karma is looking for an escape route. It wants to blame someone else.

STEPPING STONE

MAY
12

Whether life has been a good deal or a bad deal, if you have a larger purpose, everything is a stepping stone for your ultimate well-being.

MAY 13

NATURAL

Whatever the majority of people do, they say it is natural.

MAY 14

HEAVENLY

Most people's problem is not a life that is hellish, but a life that is too heavenly!

QUESTIONS

MAY 15

Very few questions have ever been truly new. Contexts and specifics may change, but the need to make sense of a world of pain and injustice stays relevant, while the human thirst to fathom the mysteries of life will endure until the end of time.

SHIRKING RESPONSIBILITY

MAY 16

Our life is of our making. What incredible freedom this spells! And yet what devious ways we have found to absolve ourselves of that responsibility.

“

LIFE BY ITSELF IS NOT COMPLICATED. IF YOU ARE NOT TRYING TO PUSH THE WORLD IN ANY WAY, IF YOU ARE JUST FINE WITH WHATEVER YOU ARE EATING AND DRINKING, WHERE IS IT COMPLICATED. IT IS ONLY YOUR MEMORY THAT COMPLICATES EVERYTHING.

”

LIBERATING

MAY 17

We must decide in our lives whether we want truth that is liberating or fancy lies that give solace.

UNIVERSAL

MAY 18

What is the way of the Divine? The way of the Divine is that there is no individuality. It is a universal process.

MAY
19

LOVING AWARENESS

When awareness arises within you, love and compassion will be the natural follow-up. When you're very loving, you are very aware.

MAY
20

CHOOSE YOUR COURSE

The significance of being a human is that you have the ability to discriminate and choose the course of your life.

SENSITIVE

MAY 21

We have to become sensitive to life—not to our thoughts, emotions, egos, ideologies, or belief systems. Because life is the highest value.

IMAGININGS

MAY 22

Human beings suffer their own memory and imagination—that is, they suffer that which does not exist.

MAY
23

LIKES AND DISLIKES

With firm likes and dislikes, you shut your doors to the many possibilities of life.

MAY
24

EXUBERANCE

Living an exuberant life is only possible when you are able to dance upon the uncertainties of life.

STRIVE

MAY 25

If you are content with who you are right now, you are not aware of who you could be if you were willing to strive.

WILLINGNESS

MAY 26

I want you to remember that what is happening within us—it does not matter for what reason it is happening—is being created by us. If we are willing, we can change that too.

MAY 27

VIRTUE

Virtue is not about practicing morality. The greatest virtue is to be inclusive of all Life.

MAY 28

LEADER

Being a leader does not mean dominating the situation. It means empowering people to do what they would not have imagined possible.

JOY

MAY 29

Joy is not an achievement. It should be the natural ambience of your life.

LESSONS

MAY 30

For a committed person, there is no such thing as failure—just lessons to be learned on the way.

MAY

31

ENERGIES

Whatever you need will just happen if you keep your energies exuberant and focused.

June

JUNE 1

A GLORIOUS SUNRISE

Every day, you are gifted with a glorious sunrise and a glorious sunset. Life is happening. You are alive. What more do you want?

JUNE 2

REALITY

By itself, reality is simple. It is ignorance that makes it complex.

THE ABYSS

JUNE 3

The abyss need not conjure dark images of a terrifying pit. It signifies a space free of all hurt and suffering, a dimension that leaves you not as an individual but as all-encompassing infinite nature, in a stillness beyond bliss.

SOURCE

JUNE 4

The very source of creation is within you. You just need to strive to make the necessary contact with it.

JUNE
5

BOUNDLESS

There is something within every human being that dislikes boundaries, that is longing to become boundless.

JUNE
6

HUMAN NATURE

Human nature is such that we always yearn to be something more than what we are right now. No matter how much we achieve, we still want to be something more. This longing is not for more—this longing is for All.

RESPOND CONSCIOUSLY

JUNE 7

The choice is always before you: to *respond consciously* to the present or to *react compulsively* to it.

DIALOGUE

Life is not an independent, self-contained bubble but a moment-to-moment dialogue with the universe.

JUNE 9

UNBINDING

The ropes that bind you and the walls that block you—these are one hundred percent of your own making. And these are all you need to unknot and dismantle.

JUNE 10

MORTAL NATURE

You discover an indescribable profundity within yourself when you realize your mortal nature. If you have not realized your eternal nature, you must at least realize your mortal nature.

CONCLUSIONS

JUNE
11

An idiot is incapable of drawing conclusions. A mystic is unwilling to draw conclusions. The rest have glorified their conclusions as knowledge.

SANCTITY

JUNE
12

Every breath, every simple act, thought, and emotion can acquire the stance of the sacred if conducted with recognition of the sanctity of the other involved—whether a person or a foodstuff or an object that you use.

JUNE 13

KARMA

Karma is the basis of your individuality, but it is also the basis of your prejudice.

JUNE 14

RESTFULNESS

The paradox is that the basis of activity is in restfulness. Action that is born of restlessness is life-taking, not life-giving. It destroys a human being in the process.

THE BODY

JUNE 15

The body has its own memory.

GATHERING

JUNE 16

People who are gathering knowledge always think they are better than people who are gathering money or things, but it is not so. It is just a question of taste. Everybody is gathering whatever is dominant in them.

JUNE 17

GURU

I believe that the whole effort of the Guru should be to help a seeker deepen his seeking, not to give him answers.

JUNE 18

ENEMIES

Competitors are not enemies. They are people who keep reminding you of your own shortcomings. Your quality control.

ENHANCE

JUNE 19

The best thing you can do for your family, your children, society, and the world around you is to enhance yourself.

IN TOUCH

JUNE 20

Devotion is a way to merge into all that you are in touch with—breath, work, people, planet, and the very universe.

JUNE 21

WHO YOU ARE

When things go wrong in life, that is when it shows who you are. When things go well, everyone can pretend to be fantastic.

JUNE 22

TRUE COMPASSION

True compassion is not giving or taking. True compassion is just doing what is needed.

“

MAN HAS BEEN GATHERING, GATHERING, AND GATHERING—EITHER THINGS, PEOPLE, OR KNOWLEDGE, HE WANTS TO GATHER. THE NEED FOR GATHERING HAS COME BECAUSE THERE IS A SENSE OF INADEQUACY AND INCOMPLETENESS.

”

JUNE 23

DIVINITY

Religious nuts have exported everything that is beautiful about a human being to the other world. They speak of divine love, divine bliss, and divine peace. Love, bliss, and peace are all human qualities. Why export these to heaven.

JUNE 24

SPIRITUAL PRACTICE

Spiritual practice is like food. Food works only for those who eat it. Spiritual practice works only for those who do it.

THE CASCADE

JUNE 25

As soon as you seek to freeze or grasp or manipulate the great roaring cascade of life, you have to stand apart from it.

SPIRITUAL GROWTH

JUNE 26

The body has its own attitudes, its own resistance, its own temperament. The body can become a means for your spiritual growth, or it can become a barrier.

JUNE 27

TOMORROW

If you do not liberate yourself from it, yesterday will rule your tomorrow. Yesterday ruling your tomorrow means tomorrow never comes.

JUNE 28

ANNIHILATION

Enlightenment means a conscious annihilation of yourself.

PRAYERS

JUNE 29

Ninety-five percent of prayers are all about asking for something, fundamentally for protection or for being taken care of. There's nothing spiritual about it—it is basic survival. In most people, the very basis of prayer is fear, insecurity, and guilt.

GRATITUDE

JUNE 30

Gratitude is not an attitude. Gratitude is something that flows out of you when you are overwhelmed by the recognition of what you have received.

July

THE PATH

JULY
1

The path by itself is not complicated. The complexities that one encounters on the spiritual path aren't because of the path. The complexities are there only because of the mess that is your mind.

ILLUSORY EXPERIENCE

JULY
2

You have built a whole cocoon of illusory experiences around yourself. Using the sense organs and the mind, you have built a very nice coating around yourself, which makes you believe that nonsense because it is experientially true.

JULY 3

CHILDHOOD

When you were a child, you were bursting with joy. Someone had to make you miserable. Today, someone has to make you happy.

JULY 4

SABOTAGE

Whether you have anger, hatred, jealousy, or resentment against someone, essentially it only works against you.

DISCOVERY

"I do not know" is not a negative state of mind. Every discovery has come from this realization.

CLARITY

Confidence without clarity is always a disaster.

JULY 7

MAINSPRING

Pain is an opportunity to bring awareness for you to investigate what is wrong. If you simply pop a painkiller without attending to the cause, the mainspring of the ailment will keep growing, and one day, it will strike even harder.

JULY 8

MANIFEST

In the end, who you are is what will manifest in the world.

SIMPLY LIFE

Become like the earth, like the tree—simply life. If you are simply life, your human consciousness will naturally find expression.

BALANCE

The simplest way to bring balance to your thoughts and emotions is unwavering commitment toward something.

JULY 11

HUMAN-CENTRIC

The universe is not human-centric. Every life-form has a role to play—that is the beauty of it.

JULY 12

BOUNDLESSNESS

Once you experience boundlessness, the possibilities in your life also become boundless.

LOVE AND LUST

JULY 13

Do you know the difference between love and lust? Lust is a strong need. Love is not a need. When you love, you settle down; nothing more is needed.

FATE

JULY 14

What you call fate is just a life situation you have created for yourself unconsciously. Your destiny is what you have crafted in unawareness.

“I want you to understand that when your parent, child, or friend is dead, you can neither care for them nor can you be uncaring toward them. Both these things are only for the living. In other words, they have crossed a boundary, beyond which it is not your realm or business.”

SELF-TRANSFORMATION

JULY 15

Self-transformation is achieved not by morals or ethics or behavioral changes, but by experiencing the limitless nature of who we are. Self-transformation means nothing of the old remains.

INFINITE

JULY 16

We are all seeking to become infinite. The only problem is that we are seeking it in installments.

JULY
17

BONDING

The question is how to make physical memory supportive rather than entangling; how to ensure, in short, that a bond does not turn into bondage.

JULY
18

PHENOMENON

You must decide if, for you, life is an account book or a phenomenon. If it is an account book, numbers matter. If it is a phenomenon of experience, then numbers don't matter.

WAY OF NATURE

JULY 19

Smartness is only socially valuable. Intelligence is the way of nature.

UNCONSCIOUS

JULY 20

When you're unconscious, where you go is not your choice. Even a dead leaf goes somewhere, but where? It cannot decide. The wind will decide.

JULY
21

TENDENCIES

Anything that is karmic dissolves only when the discerning mind is in function. If you just leave it unexamined, it hardens into a tendency.

JULY
22

AWARENESS

Mental alertness is not awareness. Awareness is a far deeper dimension.

LIVING BEING

JULY

23

Do you want to be a living being or a thinking being? Right now, ninety percent of the time, you are only thinking about life, not living it. Have you come into this world to experience life or to think about it?

SURVIVAL

JULY

24

Somehow, for a human being, life doesn't seem to end with survival; life *begins* with survival.

JULY 25

TECHNOLOGY

Yoga is a technology. If you learn to use it, it works—no matter where you come from or what you believe in or do not believe in.

JULY 26

INWARD

If you turn inward, you will find a space where there is a solution for everything.

DEATH

JULY 27

People think that death is a tragedy. It is not. People living their entire lives without experiencing life is a tragedy.

BORN AGAIN

JULY 28

Now, if you have to be born once again, you must die first. This does not mean dying physically. But if you die the way you are, if you destroy everything that you called "myself," then you become twice born or a Dwija.

JULY 29

COMPARISON

When you realize that all your material achievements are of value only in comparison with those who don't have them, this is joy that springs from another's deprivation. Can you really call it joy? Isn't it actually a kind of sickness?

JULY 30

LIVING TEMPLES

When people in the world are too distracted and unwilling to make themselves into living temples, building stone temples becomes a necessity.

EASE

JULY

31

Everything comes from the same source. You come to absolute ease only if you experience yourself as a part of existence, not as a separate individual.

August

EMPTY-HANDED

AUG
1

Whatever happens in your life, you did not come here with an investment. You came empty-handed. You cannot lose in this life.

COMPULSIONS

AUG
2

The moment you wait before you engage in a compulsion, you are aligning yourself with the conscious nature of existence. Over time, this helps weaken the compulsive nature of your behavior.

AUG 3

AVOIDANCE

If you avoid any experience—whether pain or pleasure, sorrow or joy—it is big karma. But if you go through the experience without resisting it, the karma dissolves.

AUG 4

DEPTH

The very purpose of life is to experience life in its fullest depth and dimension.

ROOTS

The roots of the Divine are entrenched in this body. If you nurture the roots, how can you avoid the flowering . . .

INNER NATURE

AUG
6

Whether you experience stress, anger, fear, or any other kind of negativity, there is only one basic cause: being ignorant of your inner Nature.

AUG 7

LIVING EXPERIENCE

Truth is neither a destination nor a conclusion. Truth is a living experience.

AUG 8

ACCESS

Life has left everything open for you. Existence has not blocked anything for anyone. If you are willing, you can access the whole universe. There *is* no door. It is open. You just have to walk through, that's all.

BIOLOGY

AUG
9

You do not have to make biology sacred, nor do you have to make it filthy. It is the instrument of life. Because of it you exist. If you know how to live it without elevating it or making it ugly, it has a beauty of its own.

SACRIFICE

AUG
10

Giving up something for something else is commerce; giving up something for nothing is sacrifice.

AUG
11

UNCONSCIOUS ACTION

Your unconscious action today will lead to consequences that compel your actions tomorrow, a year later, or even a lifetime later. No matter what you do, life will drive you into a place where you have to act.

AUG
12

POLARITIES

It is best not to create polarities within yourself. That makes for civil war and schizophrenia. Thought and feeling are not different. One is dry. Another is juicy. Enjoy both.

NO HIERARCHIES

AUG 13

Be equally involved with everything without any distinction. Put away all hierarchies. If God comes before you, the same involvement; if a frog comes before you, the same involvement.

ACCEPTANCE

AUG 14

Once there is a deep acceptance of death, life will happen to you in enormous proportions.

AUG 15

ILLUSIONS

Another word for disillusionment is Enlightenment. Enlightenment is when all illusions collapse. Right now, you selectively keep some illusions and some you collapse. If everything collapses, you are Enlightened.

AUG 16

BECOMING

The more you try to be special, the more you get hurt. Just be, just melt and become part of the wind around you, the earth around you, become a part of everything.

CHOICE

AUG
17

The very process of my whole teaching is just this, to make a person aware enough, to knock him on his head and tell him that whatever he does—whether it is love or hate, anger or peacefulness—whatever he does is still by choice.

SICKNESS

AUG
18

Almost everybody is mentally sick. It's just that they are in some manageable level of sickness.

AUG 19

A CHALLENGE

Everyone can love God, as He does not demand anything from you, but to love the one next to you right now costs life. It is a challenge. It takes much courage to do this.

AUG 20

ENCUMBERANCE

If you do not encumber your intellect with any identifications—body, gender, family, qualifications, society, race, caste, creed, community, nation, even species—you travel naturally toward your ultimate nature.

A PAINT SMEAR

AUG
21

That's all the whole of creation is: a paint smear. It starts out really thick and gross, becomes thinner and thinner and thinner, and becomes nothing.

TASTED LIFE

AUG
22

If you have tasted life, if you have known and experienced some sense of depth to it, you will know that meddling with it is the most foolish thing to do because you can't make it any more beautiful.

AUG
23

DISRUPTION

When an enlightened person is alive, they will disturb everything in your lives, but dead saints are always wonderful.

AUG
24

ROOTED

The body keeps you rooted to nature. The body *is* nature; the mind takes you far away from nature.

“

MOST PEOPLE ARE ON AND OFF IN CREATING SUFFERING, AND MOST PEOPLE ARE ON AND OFF IN CREATING LIBERATION ALSO. TO STAY ON CONSISTENTLY IS THE WHOLE THING. IF YOU STAY ON WITH SUFFERING FOR TOO LONG, IT WILL TAKE YOU TO REALIZATION IN SOME WAY, OR IT WILL DESTROY YOU.

”

AUG 25

A LITTLE BIT OF SENSE

A human being who is joyful, responsible, with a little bit of sense, can deal with challenging situations much better than those who are dead serious about everything.

AUG 26

PURPOSE

People who are bursting with life do not need a purpose to live. Life is a purpose unto itself.

INTERIORITY

AUG 27

Love is never between two people. It is what happens within you, and your interiority need not be enslaved to someone or something else.

HALLUCINATION

AUG 28

Memory and imagination are essential for survival. But there is a difference between using the mind and being used by it. It is time to stop being ruled by a hallucination and tyrannized by a dream.

AUG 29

A WAY IN

Do not look for a way out of misery. Do not look for a way out of suffering. There is only one way—and that is *in*.

AUG 30

INTENSITY

Your energy and your awareness are directly connected. If your energies are intense, your awareness naturally grows and sharpens.

SUFFERING

AUG
31

A vast number of people live in states of constant anxiety and depression. Some are suffering their failure, but, ironically, many are suffering the consequences of their success. Some are suffering their limitations, but many are suffering their freedom.

September

BLISSFUL

The very life within you is longing to be Blissful, because Blissfulness is the nature of the source of creation.

BLOSSOMING

Enlightenment happens quietly, like the blossoming of a flower.

SEP
3

GATHERED

What you consider to be your body is what you have gathered through ingestion. What you consider to be your mind is what you have gathered through the five senses. What is beyond that—which you did not gather—is who you *are*.

SEP
4

FULL-TIME

The question is: Do you want to be a full-time human being, or a part-time human being?

CONSCIOUS EXPRESSION

SEP
5

Most people are not aware of the nature of their longing. When their longing finds *unconscious* expression, we call this greed, conquest, ambition. When their longing finds *conscious* expression, we call this yoga.

FIRST GIFT

SEP
6

The most intimate part of physical creation for all of us is our own bodies. The physical body is the first gift of which we are aware.

SEP 7

FEAR

People are beginning to think that fear is a natural part of their existence. No. Fear is a result of the incompleteness of your existence. If you have limited yourself to the physical body, fear is a natural consequence.

SEP 8

BORDERLESS UNITY

Yoga is a journey toward a reality in which you experience the ultimate nature of existence as *borderless unity*. It is important to remember that this borderless unity is an experience, not an idea, philosophy, or concept.

OUT OF PLACE

Nothing has ever been out of place in this existence. Things have been out of place only in human societies.

DEVOTEE

SEP 10

A devotee is someone who is willing to dissolve into the object of devotion. If you are a devotee of life, you will become one with it. Don't be an outsider to the life process. Become a devotee. Dissolve.

SEP
11

CARRIED

If there is total clarity, there is no need for courage because clarity will carry you across.

SEP
12

HABIT INTO CHOICE

With a little awareness, every human being can begin to transform habit into choice, compulsion into consciousness.

DETACHMENT

SEP
13

Philosophies of detachment are essentially joyless creeds. Embracing them might produce some semblance of balance and stability in day-to-day life, but they do not lead to liberation.

BOUNDARY

SEP
14

When a boundary becomes too comfortable, it is time to start becoming vigilant.

SEP 15

LIVING WISDOM

What we call knowledge is frozen, accumulated memory. Knowing, on the other hand, is a dynamic process; it is living wisdom, not dead information.

SEP 16

ONLY YOU

Acceptance is freedom from the blame game, freedom from the drama of "othering," freedom from the dance of duality. There is only you in this moment and no one else. Who then can you possibly blame?

NEW FORMS

SEP 17

Transformation means that you lose your original form and are completely willing to take on new forms.

CREATION

SEP 18

This is reality, the most spectacular magic of creation.

“

WHAT IS MINE IS JUST AN EXTENDED ME. ISN’T IT. THE VERY REASON WHY, ON THE SPIRITUAL PATH, ALL POSSESSIONS ARE TAKEN AWAY, IS SO THAT WHAT IS ‘ME’ BECOMES SMALL INSIDE THIS FLESH. THE WHOLE SPIRITUAL PROCESS IS TO REMOVE THE IDENTIFICATION EVEN WITH THE PHYSICAL BODY.

”

SOUL

SEP 19

There is no such thing as "my air," but when you hold it in your lungs, it becomes you for that little period of time. So that limited aspect of the Divine that you hold within you, you call your soul.

LIFE AND DEATH

SEP 20

If you are aware, you will see both life and death are happening every moment.

SEP 21

SECURITY

Most people who claim to be seekers are seeking only security, solace, or the fulfillment of their desires.

SEP 22

MADNESS

No one can make you sane. From unmanageable madness, they can bring you down to manageable madness. Spirituality is not about moving into manageable madness. It's about going beyond the Mind that you become sane.

NIRVANA

SEP 23

The process of dissolution is going to that point where you drop all tendencies and become pure energy. When you become pure, life-making energy without attributes, we say you are Godlike. That is absolute dissolution. That is ultimate liberation.

UNTOUCHED

SEP 24

The miracle that I am, the miracle that I want to manifest on this planet, is that it is possible to be involved and engaged in this world and yet remain untouched by it.

SEP 25

THE NEED

It does not matter what you are eating, how you are, or how long you live; at some point a need will come that will make you want to get in touch with the source of Creation.

SEP 26

THOUGHTS AND EMOTIONS

The only thing that stands between you and your well-being is a simple fact: You have allowed your thoughts and emotions to take instruction from the outside rather than within.

KNOWING

SEP
27

If your seeking becomes intense enough, knowing is not far away.

EVERY PERSON

SEP
28

Don't look at anybody based on what they are right now. There is so much behind every person. It could be good and it could be bad, it could be positive and it could be negative, but there is so much behind every person.

SEP 29

DIVINE PLAN

There are those who say, "This is all a divine plan," when looking at the plight of people around them. They can talk this kind of philosophy because their stomachs are full and their lives are comfortable.

SEP 30

INVOLVEMENT

In deep, conscious involvement with everything around you, there is no entanglement, there is just joy.

October

OCT
1

BEYOND LOGIC

What I want to offer you is not logical. So the logical dimension of what I am speaking of is a stairway to deliver you into that dimension that is beyond logic.

OCT
2

PEACE

If you get disturbed and then make yourself peaceful, that's not peace—it's just a lull. Our meditations are not about peace. They're about blasting yourself until there's no peace and no disturbance in you; only that can be called peace.

YOURSELF

OCT 3

Really, the only thing that is truly worth knowing in this existence is yourself. If you know yourself, everything that is worth knowing is there within you.

FLUID ENERGY

OCT 4

When energy is stuck, identified with the body, nothing much can be done—only thoughts, emotions, and physical actions. Once the energy is free from physical identification and fluid, unimaginable things can be done with it.

OCT 5

ULTIMATE INTELLIGENCE

It is life that is the ultimate intelligence. Human intellect is mere smartness that ensures survival. But true intelligence is just life—and that which is the source of life. Nothing else.

OCT 6

HUMANITY

If your humanity overflows, Divinity will follow and serve you. It has no other choice.

ENDINGS

OCT 7

Death is not the end of life. Death is simply the end of the body. If you have lived with a very deep identification with the physical, the more you will struggle with death.

INTENTION

OCT 8

The accumulation of karma is determined by your intention, not merely by its impact on someone else.

OCT
9

HARMONIOUS

Whichever image you think is most harmonious, closest to Divinity, and closest to Realization, is the action you choose. Every moment, do it with tremendous intensity, without a break. Then a day will come when action is no longer needed.

OCT
10

ALIVE

Someday, when science goes far enough, they will find that there is nothing in the Cosmos that is not alive. The important question is: Are you alive enough to perceive it?

RAISING THE DEAD

OCT 11

Most people are living like the dead anyway because they are unconscious of many things within themselves. If people are living unconsciously, it is as good as death. So, in a way, the whole spiritual process is about raising the dead.

HEAVEN AND HELL

OCT 12

A spiritual seeker is not interested in going to heaven. They want to go to neither hell nor heaven. They want to go beyond this duality of heaven and hell.

OCT 13

ALIGNMENT

Awareness is a process of inclusiveness, embracing the entire existence. Trying to be aware will not work, but you can set the right conditions if you align your body, thoughts, emotions, and energies; awareness will blossom.

OCT 14

PRECARIOUS

So, as long as your inner life is enslaved to external situations, it will remain a precarious condition. There is no other way for it to be.

“

IN SOME WAY, THE FOOD THAT YOU EAT, THE AIR THAT YOU BREATHE, HAS GOTTEN INTEGRATED AND HAS STARTED FUNCTIONING AS A PHYSICAL BODY, AND YOU CALL THAT 'ME.' BECAUSE YOU CALL THAT 'ME,' IT IS FUNCTIONING IN A LIMITED WAY. IF YOU DO NOT CALL IT YOU, THEN IT WILL FUNCTION IN AN ENORMOUS WAY.

”

OCT
15

STUCK

One who is stuck in the realm of right and wrong, liking and disliking, will never know the texture of love.

OCT
16

HUMAN EQUATION

The human equation was always meant to be like this: to move from being to doing to having. We act in order to express our fulfillment, not to acquire it. We act in order to celebrate our inner completeness, not to pursue it.

KARMIC MEMORY

OCT 17

The problem with karmic memory is that *it has stuck to you*. If everything that passes by sticks to this mirror, it is a no-good mirror. Your mirror can no longer show you life the way it is.

LIMITATIONS

OCT 18

Do not aspire for enlightenment. The aspiration should be to grow beyond your present limitations quickly.

OCT
19

DEALING WITH DEATH

You should live your life in such a way that if you were to drop dead the next moment, you would still have ended it reasonably well. Trying to deal with death at the last moment is not the way.

OCT
20

MEANING OF LIFE

Life is about Consciousness—not concerns, compulsions, or conflict.

MORTAL

OCT 21

Once you become aware that you are mortal, you will not be dead serious about anything, but eager to live as intensely as possible.

YOUR UNIVERSE

OCT 22

You must understand that there is no such thing as your Universe. Your Universe is an illusion. This is why I bless everybody: The sooner you are disillusioned, the better it is for you.

OCT
23

CHANGING

People are no longer sensitive to what their body expresses on a daily basis. The body keeps changing all the time—even on a day-to-day basis, even within the day, the body is changing.

OCT
24

EXPERIENCE LIFE

Let everything that is life happen to you.

PAUSE

You do not need to call for angelic help or astral guidance. You simply need to pause. You will find that your mind and body work miraculously after this, because you gave your system the necessary time to fix and re-draw itself the way it wants.

GOOD AND BAD

OCT
26

As far as the law of existence is concerned, there is no good and bad, no crime and punishment. It is just that for every action, there is a consequence.

OCT
27

FOCUS

What your consciousness is intensely focused on is what will manifest in your life and in the world around you.

OCT
28

LIBERATION

When your actions are no longer about you, when they are simply based on the demands of the situation, when narrow self-interest no longer fuels your volition, you have reached the end of karmic production. Your liberation is assured.

FRESHLY BAKED

OCT 29

Suffering has to be freshly baked every day.

THE BEYOND

OCT 30

In the stillness of your mind lie perception and intelligence of the Beyond.

OCT
31

AUTONOMOUS

You are a small outcrop of this planet, prancing around and claiming to be an autonomous entity. But since you are a small extension of the Earth, whatever happens to the planet happens to you too.

November

NOV
1

THE CREATOR

That is all it takes to touch the Creator—just willingness, nothing else.

NOV
2

DYNAMISM AND STILLNESS

A spiritual person is *one who has found action in inaction, and inaction in action.* Spirituality is about dynamism and stillness cohabiting within you to give you a taste of living death all the time.

GAME OF LIFE

NOV 3

All the various manifestations that you see as life today are fundamentally rooted in duality. Because there are two, there are many. Once there are two, the game of life begins.

KARMA AND SUFFERING

NOV 4

Karma is the only concept in the world that addresses human perplexity in the face of suffering. It is the only logic that explains the seeming arbitrariness of the world we live in.

NOV 5

UNSULLIED

Selective involvement leads to suffering and Karma; detachment leads to lifelessness. When your action is unsullied by past impressions, it is liberating.

NOV 6

AGING

With age, physical agility may diminish, but the level of joy and aliveness need not. If your level of joy and aliveness is declining, you are committing suicide in installments.

ANGUISH

NOV 7

You are the manufacturer of your own anguish.

LIKES AND DISLIKES

NOV 8

There is a certain New Age impulse to speak of positive and negative energy somewhat indiscriminately. It usually means that people have likes and dislikes and have not yet transcended them.

NOV 9

EXPRESSION OF BLISS

When you operate out of a state of inner fulfillment rather than inner hankering, your life becomes an expression of bliss, not a pursuit of it.

NOV 10

SEESAW

Inward projection of life energies gives you organic unity and stability of life. Outward projection gives you a strong presence and expression of life. This seesaw is naturally happening with all life, including human beings.

UNNATURAL

NOV 11

This morbid fear of death is not natural. Death is a natural process. If life happens, then death is natural. Being afraid of something natural is unnatural.

EFFORTLESS

NOV 12

Devotion is not an act, it is not directed toward one thing or another; the *object* of devotion is immaterial. It is just that with devotion you have dissolved all the resistance in you so that the Divine can transpire as effortlessly as breath.

NOV 13

RIDE THE CYCLE

Anything that is physical, from the atomic to the cosmic, is cyclical. Either you ride the cycle or you are crushed by it.

NOV 14

FOLLY

One of the biggest human follies is to engage with death in the third person, as though it is an abstract event that happens to other people, not us.

INTERNAL CYCLE

NOV
15

Karma is not some external system of crime and punishment. It is an internal cycle generated by you. These patterns are not oppressing you from without, but from *within.*

SPIRITUALITY

NOV
16

Spirituality happens only because you paid attention to your life and you saw that you don't know where it begins and where it ends.

"

YOU MUST UNDERSTAND THAT THE ENERGY HAS NO QUALITY OF ITS OWN. IT IS NEITHER POSITIVE NOR NEGATIVE, NEITHER GOOD NOR BAD. IT JUST FUNCTIONS BY TENDENCIES. GOOD AND BAD QUALITIES ARISE WITHIN YOU ONLY WHEN DISCRETION ARISES. WHERE THERE IS NO DISCRETION, THERE IS NO POSITIVE AND NEGATIVE.

"

YOUR PAST

NOV 17

You believe you are an individual because your memory tells you that this is who you are. Think about it. Everything you consider to be yourself is a result of memory. What you call "me" is a product—in every sense of the term—of your past.

CRIPPLING

NOV 18

Once you set this condition that "Life should happen the way I think it should happen," you are setting up a crippling process—you will do less and less in the world, because the more you attempt, the fewer things happen your way.

NOV 19

A WAY FORWARD

Yoga is a system where it doesn't matter what kind of a fool you are, what level of unawareness you're in, what kind of karmic bondages you have, there's still a way for you.

NOV 20

DIVERGENCE

The mind is a great divergence. It can go anywhere. You can train it to go anywhere. You can take it in any direction, far away from Truth.

NOV 21

BORROWED

The physical body is something that you have borrowed from the planet on which you're living. When the time comes, the planet will reclaim your body. The planet won't let you keep even an atom of it. You have to shed it totally.

NOV 22

DISCERNMENT

When the mind encounters memory, a certain amount of discernment is involved. But the body takes on memory without discernment. It simply receives.

NOV
23

FRAGILITY

When your very body perceives the fragility of its existence, there is a very profound relief and acceptance.

NOV
24

FREEDOM SEEKER

The goal for every freedom seeker is the same: to attend to your karma *now* rather than wait for life to throw it at you.

COSMIC NATURE

NOV 25

If you know this piece of life, you know everything worth knowing in this cosmos, because the cosmic nature has happened the way this piece of life has happened. You don't have to search the whole cosmos to know the mysteries of the universe.

IN YOUR HANDS

NOV 26

If you compulsively react, external situations determine how you are right now. If you consciously respond, your well-being is very much in your hands.

NOV 27

UNWAVERING

Once you are constantly aware of your mortality, your spiritual search will be unwavering.

NOV 28

DUTY

The idea of duty comes from the moral systems we have created in case our humanity fails. As a Guru, I want every individual's humanity to be active every moment, rather than work on a fallback system that merely mimics humanity.

GENETIC MEMORY

NOV 29

You need genetic memory for survival, continuity, and well-being, but you also need a distance from it to live a life of consciousness, joy, and freedom.

HUMAN INTELLIGENCE

NOV 30

Once you have come with the human form, life has given you a certain sense of intelligence, awareness, and freedom to choose what you want to be right now, in this moment. Every human being has this within them.

December

AN ALTERNATIVE

DEC 1

You don't have a choice about being in pain, but you do have a choice about suffering. You can always choose *not* to suffer.

SEEDS

DEC 2

The effect is only an indicator of the problem; by merely erasing it, you are only enabling the seeds of the problem to manifest in some other way.

DEC
3

THE DIFFERENCE

Whatever you do in unawareness, you can also do in awareness. That is the difference between ignorance and enlightenment.

DEC
4

IGNORANCE

Ignorance is also a karma. As action is karma, inaction is also karma!

TEACHINGS

DEC 5

A teaching, after a certain period of time, becomes a block by itself. You will twist it to your convenience. This is counterproductive because a teaching is not meant to support you, it is meant to demolish you!

UNBOUNDEDNESS

DEC 6

If you have tasted the unboundedness in you, if you truly experienced yourself beyond the limitations of the physical and the mental, there would be no fear.

DEC 7

FUNDAMENTAL

Peace is not the highest goal in life. It is the most fundamental requirement.

DEC 8

LAP OF TRUTH

If you are truly a seeker of Truth, Truth cannot hide from you. It is in the lap of Truth that you have happened.

SWEETEST EMOTION

Devotion is the sweetest emotion you can nurture within yourself.

IN YOUR HANDS

Once you have taken one part of your life into your hands, you cannot leave another part to somebody else.

DEC 11

TRAP OF INTELLECT

The first step toward moving from the trap of the intellect to the lap of a larger intelligence is to recognize that every aspect of life—atomic to cosmic—is a manifestation of a far greater intelligence than your minuscule intellect.

DEC 12

ONE MOMENT

If you go outward, it is an endless journey. If you turn inward, it is just one moment.

PHYSICALITY

DEC 13

Simple compulsions, whether of hunger or lust, can rule you so strongly that they will not allow you to look beyond the physical. It is easy to forget that the physical body is only *a part* of you; it is important that it does not become the whole of you.

YEARNING

DEC 14

A genuine seeker who develops an urge within will always find his Guru. He may find it in a man, in a woman, or even in a rock. He will find it somewhere. When any being calls or really yearns, existence answers.

DEC
15

WHOLENESS

What we call feeling healthy is having a sense of wholeness within us. Just being free of diseases medically is not health. If we feel like a complete human being in our body, mind, and spirit, that is when we are really healthy.

DEC
16

CREATE LOVE

You do not have to create love. If you recognize the contribution that everyone is making for you, love will arise within you.

UNCOMFORTABLE

DEC 17

Being with a Master is never comfortable, because He will break all your limitations, all your ideologies.

ALL-CONSUMING

DEC 18

All the life-denying philosophies of detachment have developed because of the human fear of entanglement. What these philosophies overlook is that without an all-consuming, passionate involvement, there would be no life.

DEC 19

HUNGRY

You can't talk spirituality to a man who is hungry on the street; it won't mean anything to him. A culture that is new is hungry, hungry for life and well-being, because people still remember the difficulties their forefathers went through to build it.

DEC 20

THE FAMILIAR

The attraction to one's own karmic patterns can be powerful, because most people experience a sense of safety in the familiar.

STRUGGLE

DEC 21

You and every human being live in a constant struggle between the physical and the dimension beyond the physical. Though you have the compulsiveness of the physical, you also have the consciousness of being more than just physical.

PAST LIFETIMES

DEC 22

Don't waste your time and life digging into the past. Most people are unable to handle the memories, thoughts, and emotions of one lifetime. So opening many will not bring well-being.

DEC 23

EXISTENCE

If you just sit here, your whole being will pulsate with existence. There's no other way to Be.

DEC 24

LETHARGY

A man who does not know action—real action, intense action—can never move into inaction. If you try to, inaction will just become lethargy.

WHAT IS NEEDED

DEC
25

That is what awareness means—there is no volition. Where there is no volition, there is no Karma. Whatever you are doing is just happening as it is needed.

EVOLVE

DEC
26

When you are miserable, you long for heaven, not liberation. The longing for liberation arises only when life is good, but you naturally want to evolve to the next dimension.

DEC
27

DISTANCE YOURSELF

Becoming free of memory and losing your memory are two different things. We want to distance ourselves from our memory. We don't want to lose it, we just want to carry it a bit loosely on us.

DEC
28

LOOK

Don't look for anything. Don't look for the meaning of life. Don't look for God. *Just look*—that's all.

A PIECE OF OUR PLANET

DEC 29

Everything that ever happened on this planet is remembered by your body, because your body is just a piece of this planet.

NOW

DEC 30

If you are conscious, there is only one place in which you can be. Now.

DEC
31

THE CAGE

The life and work of every spiritual guide, across history and across cultures, has been just this: to point out that the cage door does not exist. Whether you choose to fly or choose to remain within the limitations of the cage—let that be a conscious choice.

Reflect

HARMONY BOOKS
An imprint of Random House
A division of Penguin Random House LLC
1745 Broadway, New York, NY 10019
harmonybooks.com | randomhousebooks.com
penguinrandomhouse.com

The quotes in this work were originally published as follows: in the following titles self-published by Sadhguru: *Enlightenment: An Inside Story* and *Mystic's Musings;* in the following titles by Sadhguru published by Harmony Books, an imprint of Random House, a division of Penguin Random House LLC: *Death* (2025), *Inner Engineering* (2016), and *Karma* (2021); or, on the author's website, isha.sadhguru.org.

ISBN 978-0-593-79727-3

Printed in Malaysia

9 8 7 6 5 4 3 2 1

First Edition

BOOK TEAM:
Editor: Michele Eniclerico
Art director: Jenny Davis
Designer: Jessie Kaye
Managing editor: Allie Fox
Production editor: Kelly Chian
Production manager: Maggie Hart

Stock images: gold and white pattern—ollyka/Shutterstock; mandala—Panda Lover/Shutterstock; vintage sunburst—Foxys Graphic/Shutterstock; lotus flower—Katika/Shutterstock

The authorized representative in the EU for product safety and compliance is Penguin Random House Ireland, Morrison Chambers, 32 Nassau Street, Dublin D02 YH68, Ireland. https://eu-contact.penguin.ie